YELP!

YELP!
Liz Almond

2009

Published by Arc Publications
Nanholme Mill, Shaw Wood Road
Todmorden OL14 6DA, UK
www.arcpublications.co.uk

Copyright © Liz Almond 2009
Design by Tony Ward
Printed in Great Britain by the MPG
Books Group, Bodmin and King's Lynn

978 1904614 38 8 pbk
978 1904614 91 3 hbk

ACKNOWLEDGEMENTS:

'Silk', 'The Man Who's Easy On The Eye Is On The Beach' and 'Rosita Rules The Roost' appeared in *Ambit*, February 2007. 'Picking Glasswort' and 'Allotment' were published by Cinnamon Press in their anthology entitled *Only Connect*, December 2007. 'A Barefoot Doctor Asks Me To Undress' was short-listed for the Keats-Shelley prize 2008.

The author is grateful to Arts Council England for an award in 2004 to support the writing of this collection.

In memory of Julia Casterton whose generosity, perspicacity and enthusiasm informed her editorial role.

The author wishes to thank everyone in her writing group for their invaluable support and insight.

This book is in copyright. Subject to statutory exception and to provision of relevant collective licensing agreements, no reproduction of any part of this book may take place without the written permission of Arc Publications.

Cover picture:
'Girl Lifting Skirt to Dog' by Paula Rego
© Copyright of the artist, photograph courtesy of
Marlborough Fine Art (London) Ltd.

The Publishers acknowledge financial
assistance from ACE Yorkshire

Editor for the UK and Ireland: John W Clarke

*A Don Riccardo,
amor mio, mi guitarrista*

Contents

Yelp / 9
Quarantine / 11
Island Quarantine / 13
Negative / 15
The Rulebook For Being Alone / 17
The Man Who's Easy On The Eye Is On The Beach / 18
Silk / 20
Satellite Cinema:
Nimiq 1 / 22
Turqsat IC / 24
Yamal 202 / 26
B-Sat 2A / 27
Beidou 1B / 29
Essaim-3 / 31
Hotbird 5 / 33
Wasp / 35
Cuckoo / 37
Birds / 38
The Moorish Gecko / 40
Rosita Rules The Roost / 42
Panic Attack / 43
Chryselephantine / 44
Bitter Water / 46
Kathakali School / 48
Malabar Must / 49
Houseboat / 51
Durga's Tiger / 52
Balancing Act / 53
Girl Almost Writing / 55

Girl Dogging / 56
Girl Reading at Window / 57
Girl In Sandpit / 58
Girl Lifting Skirt to Dog / 60
Girl Swimming / 61
Finding Your Place / 62
A Passing Phase / 63
Farouche / 65
Bushcraft / 67
Sweet Doing Nothing / 69
Scalded / 71
Fuente / 72
Gacela For The Life Of Julia / 73
Silk Purse / 74
Allotment / 75
Aperture / 76
Attention-seeking / 77
High Tea / 78
Sharon Olds Reads To The Animals / 80
Picking Glasswort / 81
Postcard From The Zone / 83
Stork Cools Wings / 84
Paper Wings / 86
A Barefoot Doctor Asks Me To Undress / 88
Huerta de San Vicente / 89
A Single Orange Was The Only Light / 90

Notes / 91
Biographical Note / 91

Yelp

> *Whatever returns from oblivion*
> *returns to find a voice*
>   Louise Gluck

The old one, irretrievable.
It took too much energy to speak,
I could hear it waver, weaken,
like a winter sun, defeated.

When you cry in the wilderness
no-one hears your animal yelp.

Could you speak up please?
But speaking up
means lying down for two hours
blanked out, listening
to other people's voices.

A petal torn,
a hank of hair pulled out,
makes your eyes water.
One day in late Autumn
when the colour is up
you can feel burnt siena
in your throat like gingerbread.
It's back! A pomegranate
bursting on its branch.

Speak only when you have
something worthwhile to say
about oblivion, and how
you returned from it,
like Lawrence in his battered boat
with his little cakes and wine
and even, dishes!

You come back from oblivion
into the arms of Demeter
with her diamond voice,
the music of pouring water,
blessed irrigation.

Quarantine

I had no need of a wall, a fence, a ha-ha,
my housebound self told me how far
I could go. I was tempted to do a runner
but house-arrest is a Burmese condition,
and anyway, I found *there is nowhere to go*
when you're in quarantine,
except further in, deeper down
as if you're a bulb, planted,
have to endure darkness
until it's time to stop at your station.

I had with me my notebook,
mobile phone, secateurs and water.
The only one who understood, my daughter
with her book of plants for situations.
Which accessory do I really want,
secateurs or pen, pen or secateurs?
It could be neither, try *give me a torch*
switch on the answer phone, retreat,
let forty days and forty nights
turn into a hundred and forty days and nights

which is far too long to survive.
I'm tempted to take up smoking,
drink whisky, venture out of bounds
onto the forbidden moor and mountain.
When I come out of solitary confinement,
I find summer has passed me by

and I've skipped a season into autumn's
dismembering, between what I was
and what I might be;
an altogether altered state.

Island Quarantine

I have quarantine fever, an island
symptom where the smell of baking bread
wakes me while it is still dark,
kindles a compulsion to walk
to the monastery,
only destination for my pilgrimage.

I arrive just as the caretaker gets up,
attends to her morning tasks.
We have no common language
except the word for thirst
and she points to a tap. Miracle.

She ushers me into the chapel,
an airless room that smells
of hot wax and burning oil.
It's as stifling as the centre of a hive
with its clutch of sealed up prayers
manifest as tin offerings, body-parts
pinned to the icon's skirts,
layer on layer, holy sequins
catching the light. Aflame.

She makes me coffee, black and Greek.
We sit at the communal supper table
in the churchyard under a cypress tree
where the air is untroubled, less volatile.
I sip, feel the sweet silt
hit my tongue. Answer to a prayer.

I leave the monastery,
pass each monk's separate cell
with its red geranium –
even God could not imagine
the redness of a red geranium,
fiery nail varnish, sole colour
in a landscape bleached
by months of sun and drought
to a wisp of wild barley
blowing in a field high above the sea.

Negative

The graveyard was swept,
tended lovingly,
although this morning
shocks me with an open coffin
thrown over the perimeter wall
with some old wreaths,
tatters of funeral fabric.

We're close to heaven
but heaven has no time
for plastic flowers or tawdry monuments
and it's obvious
the souls are drawn away
from stacked tombs that stifle them.

What's left is for the living:
consolations, comforts.
When I photograph
the fronts of tombs,
polished glass
reflects myself back
as negative, the other side
waiting to claim me,
shut me up and seal me
away from the sun.

Now I can see the point of sky burials,
the economy of pecked flesh.
Face the sun, nothing can blind you now
and it doesn't matter
if your shoes are too small.

The birds will tend you, lovingly,
devotedly, viciously,
till your bones are white as
limewash in the spring sun,
sterile as newly forged metal.

You stipulate your bones
are to be buried
under an almond tree,
high up, remote, and heavenly.

The Rulebook For Being Alone

Never take lifts from strangers
unless over-heated
and crazy for salt water.

Don't swim alone
where currents are wilful
unless you have a taste for risk.

Don't set off at dawn
without torch or whistle
unless you have an urgent journey.

You have to cross yourself
over the threshold into the vortex
of a household shrine lit up by oil.

You must cover your arms
for this is a monkish cell
even if dressed up with ribbons, dried roses.

You must tear up the rulebook
and scatter it leaf by leaf
from the highest cliff. Petals, feathers.

The Man Who's Easy On The Eye Is On The Beach

His wife has little plaits, crow's feet. She teaches
him to unlearn Albanian, adopt demotic Greek
in which he learns to curse and swear,

to flirt, sweet-talk, cook the boss's books,
how to flatter, sell and never tear
well-sealed envelopes containing words

like 'circumspect', 'discretion'.
Don't talk to her, she's on her own
you don't know what she's looking for,

if anything. She might be on the rebound
or fond of solitude, or full of grief,
she could be on the look-out

for someone with whom to correspond.
The man who's easy on the eye
has surface shimmer like gold leaf

and if it's stripped away you find
a swamp of dead brothers
the sister who jumped,

his mother's burnt bread, smouldering,
his father's broken shoulder
in its dirty sling.

This is the sealed envelope
even his mother-wife
can't prise open.

Silk

Torn silk. A way in
to the waterways
you've learned to love
and despite a fear,
you long for tracer fire
cutting horizontal pathways
across the city's temple roofs.

A rip of silk. She asks you
to let down her hair,
take out the tortoiseshell clip
that's held it up all day.
Your day began with a mosquito bite,
it marks the start
of another rainy season that leaves
damp patches on your shirt,
the shirt she unbuttons
to kiss your navel.

You've just returned from
a fox-hole with its filthy mud,
from the eye of the watchtower
below which a car-bomb explodes
and makes your shoes
shiny with someone else's blood.
You remember the cameraman
get this one, over here
leaning too close to a woman
who shields a baby in her arms.

You want to remember
a rattan table, coffee cups,
painted toenails,
hair that's yet to be undone.
You watch the boat whose unlit lantern
is a moon about to rise
out of a piece of crumpled silk.

Satellite Cinema

Nimiq 1

Blindfold or hood
prelude to captor's boot
and rupture.
My hood smells of my own breath
condensing. Bite on cloth,
remove yourself
to the old walls of the medina
which might be a place of safety
if walls can be impregnable
which I doubt.
There are jasmines, fountains,
the smell of flatbread baking.
Taste of saffron, preserved lemon
may be your salvation.

Urination. Hot on your thigh
and you believed continence
was your birthright
keeping things in,
holding on to stay intact
when you can only cry under your hood,
a child held in the geometry
of four walls.

I am pushed up some steps
and at last my hood is removed
as the plane banks.
Will I be returned to my wife
with her small machete,
her waist length hair
and silver anklet, music of freedom?
When the cabin door is opened
and out we file handcuffed together
the first sharp smell of home
wafts up from the ground
pink as dried pomegranate seed,
inside of mouths, dried blood.
Where are the antidotes to hood,
humiliation and harm?

It was the old apricot tree, *mishmish,*
that saved me, helped me wish
for ordinary happiness, eat *baba ganoush*
under its branches, watch its fruit
ripen in the sun, deepen in colour,
fall into my open hands,
warm, downy, freckled
like my daughter's face.

Turqsat 1C

They call her the translucent one
after Deglet Nour, treasure of southern oases
where she loves to watch
every cluster of blossom being
hand-pollinated till it stirs with promise.
Her beloved palm groves are ignorant
(like the Medjool) of the theatre
playing out its dramas in the north.
Later in the season she packs fruit into boxes,
rows of moth mummies waiting for night flight.
She folds waxed paper over their fragile skins
destined for a maternity ward,
its swaddle of newborns
crying for non-existent milk as if a giant straw
sucks on the hospital's vital organs.
The elders know a diet of dates
can help a mother make her own milk,
all you do is unclench your stomach,
breathe deeply, in through nose,
out through mouth, reduce adrenaline's flow,
remove yourself to an oasis
and let its waters calm you,
relax in the shade of palm leaves,
hold a date on your tongue
till it melts, till its sugars dissolve
and energise your much depleted self.

Practise lactation, rehearse the aesthetic of
sand, palm tree, opalescent water
to restore your equilibrium.
Dates on the calendar
fix beginnings, ends,
catastrophes, festivals.
At last the date stone's clean,
shuttle for miniature loom,
shape of a body wrapped.

Yamal 202

Ghamsar, day of the rose harvest.
A whole village gets up before sunrise
to gather roses drenched with dew
for proper distillation.

Not far away, some controlled explosions
look like bunches of white roses
thrown in an arc across the night,
stems shooting out their stars.

If the rose petals fall
upon a body, its skin ignites
for phosphorus feeds on air and water
with which it sharpens neural pathways.

Visibility poor in mist and fog patches
convenient smokescreens hide
what white hot roses
make of human flesh
at melting point forty four degrees centigrade.

B-Sat 2A

I can never get warm enough.
A cage of chickens would do,
if I sleep on top of their cage
the press of chicken flesh
heats me up.
But the chicken economy's sick.
Yesterday a man in rubber gloves
was wringing neck after neck
and there's a lime pit full of heaving feathers.

This may be the last time I pick lice from my chickens,
let them peck nits from my hair.
I love their yellow feet,
the way they pick them up
and tread them down again,
I think stepping is the essence of chicken.

The man in the gloves came to show me
what he saw under his microscope:
brown rods seethe in a commotion
of beads, bubbles, green and amber,
particles of virus that signal GO –
to market? to hospital?
Chickens is finished,
chicken feet burn until they're black.

I cycle back to my village
with the empty cage,
I can't get warm,
I can never get warm,
I'm shivery, finished, collapsed,
I'm burning up, I can't get warm,
I'm home but they won't let me in,
I'm in quarantine with myself.

Beidou 1B

A body more eloquent, prostrate,
arms outstretched, palms upturned
and the shadows of her fingers
lengthen, yearn for another body
whose arm, flung into the frame,
is bruised, cut, swollen;
its hand tangled in rope and seaweed
cups nothing but a gasp of air.

The woman's sandal leaves a sad imprint,
its leather inner reflects sunlight
where her heel has polished the hide.
She's been scarified and claws at sand,
ephemeral marks of fingernails
will be washed away as the beach renews.

Beside her spread sari is half a lemon,
an oil lamp and a temple bell;
they will give her hands something to do
when she hauls herself onto her feet,
slips on the sandal, feels its worn shape
mould to her again.

Fishermen drag the ruined body up the beach
like a broken boat.
Catamarans of the karamadi
return with their catch
which women begin to gut and clean
ready for the first meal
since disaster crashed into their lives,
left them huddled together
like fish in a tightening net.

Essaim-3

I learn to domesticate
what was wild
and less amenable,

its pressed oil a liquid gold
to anoint both the living
and the dead.

Steep rose petals in it
or coriander seed,
let its river meander

through you to your lungs,
their bronchioles
like spectral trees.

I rehearse another climate
where you need danger money
to get through the olive harvest;

Abdel Karim Hamad's
harvest, his oil therapy
good for liver and eyes;

eyes witness bulldozers
uprooting ancient trees,
knotty, twisted, furrowed.

Generations of fruit
ruined in one offensive
which you know you must

resist, with beseeching arm
at full stretch, chancing
it, playing the female card.

Burn it, it will survive.
Cut it down, it will sprout.
Dig it up and there's no give

only take. Cast first stone.
Accept honeycomb,
mint tea, coffee.

Hotbird 5

Not quite in my hand but on the laptop screen
the earth appears intact, pristine,
viewed from satellite Hotbird 5
far enough away to disguise
all signs of human depredation,
all attempts to over-heat,
degrade, destroy.

A different satellite, Ariane
shows mostly ocean, not a uniform blue
after all, there are spectral trails
like strings of pearls, diamonds,
underwater mountains capped with snow,
dragnets full of iridescent fish.
Ariane's gaze is unable to detect
what marine biology knows:
sewage sleeping in the mussel beds,
organophosphate pearling up oyster shells,
the altered state of polar ice caps,
an atlas melting, cracking up.

Hotbird, my virtual flight instructor,
I've grown out of trunks and carpets,
long for more altitude, thinner air,
realise the globe's fiction of blue and green
is just that. From the satellite position

see continents in relief, crinkled,
stretched, with tracts of parched land,
desert, savannah, bleached out,
and at the margins, deltas
empty into seas whose
currents swirl and eddy,
spinning water held in place by gravity.
Far enough away not to see
gunfire, explosions, implosions
as the creatures argue amongst themselves.

Wasp

I follow the buzz
to a piece of antique rosewood
where some primitive paper-making
is going on in secret.

I envy your utter concentration
as you build each fluted papier-mache cell
the colour of preserved lung.

You interrupt my breathing.
I hold on as you lower your dangerous abdomen
down into the cell to test your building technique.

Your buzz threatens, amplifies
over vast distances,
quickens my attention.

When did you start your tricks Madame?
Why is your thorax so paper thin?
What do your hideous colours suppose?

An iniquity of life beyond sting
insults the honey bee
and gives you an unwanted edge

unwanted in the late summer garden
where a split fig on a plate
invites your company.

You love meat as well as sugar,
we'll bait a jar to trap you –
maggots steeped in orange blossom honey.

Smoke is my armoury, weaponry,
it maddens you, you cover the baby basket
with your cheated body as if it were a dead child.

A sudden movement distracts you,
you dart at my bare foot
with your sting primed.

A shoe bears down on you,
there, there is your mashed belly
its black and yellow warning signs disarmed.

In a last convulsion
mouth sucks on own fully extended sting,
and her ball of dormant unused sperm
invisible to the naked eye

goes to waste. I wasted its potency,
that and the casual killing
paralyses my pen

which is like a wand, rewriting
the stigmata sting on my seven year old hand,
horror of a nest in the very next bed....

Cuckoo

The almond tree casts an iron skirt
around itself: parabola, corset.
I sat on the terrace for hours,
I knew it was hours by the way
the almond tree clock revolved
upon itself through shifting shadow.
When the skirt whirled out at nine
it was four in the afternoon,
time for swallows to gorge on flies,
time the cuckoo calls from a rock thrush's nest,
one solitary thing to another.
Mary Oliver asks
    Is the soul solid like iron?
no, it can by-pass matter,
but can't smell the bitter scent of almond
that only the skin of a living hand picks up.

Birds
for Jose Antonio Gomez de Toro

Are singing – pay attention! The lesson began
on Jose's doorstep, opposite the house
of the woman who sells us eggs and oranges.

You sing, you can't help it,
but look how your wings atrophy –
a thousand sharp notes between cage and tree.

My teacher's cage is empty, door open,
the inmate's sentence has been served:
parole, pardon, surprise release.

His birdcage is silver, electroplated,
letting slivers of moonlight
stripe the wall where a neighbour's ear is pressed,

eavesdropping. Keep your voice down
or better still, pick up your mobile phone
and text what might incriminate.

Agitate. Discriminate. The liberties you take
are not unnoticed. What you curse
can be a blessing. Pay attention!

Without the hated mast your phone
can't ring a doctor in the dead of night
when pain and peristaltic failure

call from deep inside, behind your ribcage
where all your organs sing,
automatic as birds.

Moorish Gecko

In the parched path
I have seen the good lizard
(one drop of crocodile)
meditating.
                Federico Garcia Lorca from 'The Old Lizard'

In the parched path
it was stiff and lifeless,
an arrow pointing up
beyond the eucalyptus tree.

Its white apron
newly laundered
tucked itself into the folds
of its throat,
soft pouch, working bellows
when a lizard breathes.

But now (one drop of crocodile)
as I turn its body over
and run my fingers
over its relief map back
I think of smart shoes,
handbags snapping shut.

A Moorish Gecko is good to eat
if large enough,
steamed with tomato, garlic, parsley.
It tastes of the country,
of thyme and rosemary
it's brushed against
meditating

in the parched path
on why the good lizard died,
belly up to last night's moon
which was just too bright
for its old jewelled eyes
whose lids are shut.

I have seen the good lizard
meditating
on its own parched body,
a meal for ants
parading in through
its open jaw,
round trip itinerary.

Beyond the burning light
that took its breath away
it gives me one last insight:
its skull an arrowhead
pointing me north, for
it is the hour to depart
up the parched path to safety,
to water.

Rosita Rules The Roost

She howls her way up the cobbles,
demented, bereaved, demented,
leans on her whittled stick –
pause in the syntax of scream –
until the other widows come
to lead her back to her carmen,
sit her down by the myrtle
whose white petals calm her.
She lapses into lines she learned by rote,
a sip of Manzanilla in her throat:
give me an orange or a good quince any day.

In another's country she'd be in a locked ward
subdued by a sledgehammer of drugs.
In her own, she ranges free as a chicken
waiting to have its neck wrung.

Her night screams are part of the street furniture
but not what the beautification committee had in mind,
and the English, being English,
flutter away, goldfinches frightened
from the branches of a pomegranate tree.
Las ramas, las ramas, por las ramas
her furious heels stamp out a terminal morse code.

Panic Attack

Storm clouds gather at the crossroads,
a character enters stage right from the olive grove
dressed in dark brown homespun
together with twisted turban
which may or may not conceal horns,
innocently repel rain. She could be bald
and she murmurs, oracle-like,
to the sheep and goats roped to her wrist.
The instant she puts pipe to lip
out flies a string of disturbed notes
like maddened bees looking for someone to sting.
Now the shepherdess stares us out,
clicks her little hooves together,
throws down a clutch of olive stones
onto our path, spits on them,
disappears into her past
in which she forages endlessly
for her mortal self.

Chryselephantine

Ivory poached from the river horse's mouth
makes a boy-god sublime;
he's wired in his own vitrine
for us to marvel at muscle and vein.
Boy-worship, how Greek!
I'm jealous of his speed,
the energy of gold leaf, molten,
forms a spear-shaped ingot
for greater thrust.

I look out of my window,
hear a boy crying his way to school;
inauspicious start to the day.

I am slow, slow as a sleepy terrapin
sunning itself by the cistern
where I keep my sacred boat,
model of the one I once sailed
up the Nile in.
The women of Thebes are on the mountain,
they've abandoned themselves.

I was abandoned at the palace gate,
dragged myself in my lead skirt
somnambulant down corridors
of polished jade till I arrived at the ward.
Ward? Its etymology of surveillance
makes me defensive,

shielding my eyes from the words
cardiac, paediatric, chronic.

I take my anger out on the perfect boy:
smash his face against stone,
alchemy of gold leaf flayed from his body
before the inferno reduces him to charcoal.

A shell can be an instrument if strung,
or a means of divination.
Crackled thighs pulled from ash
are oracular too.

Bitter Water

An Ambassador ferries us right to our village
where a frog greets you, grasps
the manager's sari. A telltale trickle
of blood on my leg signals one more bite,
the mosquito is a skilled anaesthetist.

In her village there is no flyscreen,
ceiling fan or toilet.
She's glossed her hair with coconut oil,
steps out onto startling white sand
pale as my skin, which fascinates
just because it's different, Meena says.
But I want to be brown, brown
as the boys who cluster too close,
clutch at my bag and clothes,
excite themselves inside their lungis.
In her village don't go walking alone
unless you're a fisherman
flinging his net to catch
a wave of silvery sardines.

I'm strolling through a communal latrine;
no-one warned you that the beach
has other complexions, other functions
which burst your myth, smash your idyll.

You've known the tropical one
forever, it seems: geography's lesson,
TV's fakery airbrushing
Miss Crusoe into paradise,
teeth wrapped round a Bounty Bar.

Kathakali School

Daily for eight whole years
I've opened the lid of my make-up box
entered each narrative
through a prologue of greasepaint and brushes.

I slowly become my character,
in skirt and head-dress,
I unfold stories like pleats in a sari,
bright, silky, edged with gold.

Now I can command the floor
as my eyeballs swivel,
dance of finger and thumb
precise as the insistent drum.

The spirit of the temple
guides my ankles, tendons pull on bone,
feet brace for the arrow to fly from bow
straight to the heart of the boar.

I long for the temple gate,
for all night ritual,
a temple audience that knows every mudra
off by heart and mimics each back to me
as the story exhausts us
and I go back behind the curtain
to recover myself.

Malabar Must

His Madness' annual pilgrimage
ends at Varkala
a place where people congregate
with their loved ones' ashes
in brass pots – scatter, fling, disperse....

His Madness sits in cobbler pose
beneath a cut lime wet emerald
paddy leaf silk umbrella,
its gold fringe a little over the top
but here on the beach
everything's surreal,
lit up like the temple lamps
we pass on our way down,
lured by a single note
sustained, held
in the mouth of His Madness,
who's all coiled muscle on bone
cobra rearing from a basket of coir.

The temple elephant
trumpets her call and response,
rattles the chain at her ankle
in sad percussion.
She's longing for a dip in the ocean,
relief from gravity.
She thinks you, my love, are her mahout,
holds her trunk for you
to climb up behind her ears

sound of cracked cardamom seed
elephant hair wiry against your thigh
smell of jasmine flower and dung.
We're lagooned in a mirage,
it leads us on and on into the rainforest
till we're altered, junglified, lost.

Houseboat

Kettuvallam rotates on its anchor
deep in green coconut water
that doubles up a three quarter moon
makes every captain's bamboo pole
twice as long as it was yesterday
like the snake boat stretched out
longing for its next race.
Sajith swims at dawn
to a jangle of temple music
moving time along
standing it still
or speeding it up
like a kingfisher in flight –
blink and I'll miss it.

Durga's Tiger

At the bottom of the temple steps
there's a rack for everyone's shoes:
mostly rubber flip flops
or sandals cut from a discarded tyre.
Trainers mark you out
the way a line of yellow paste
means you're one of Shiva's.
You press a few rupees
into the shoe-wallah's palm,
she fingers the suede as if it were
the underside of an elephant's ear
or a baby's foot.

Many lamps light your way
up to the temple gate
where Durga glares down at you,
makes sure you've washed your feet
at the temple tank below,
raises her trident and bow:
I admire her for her fierce intent,
her skill with weaponry, her energy
and solitary waywardness,
so unlike those devotees
busy at the shrine where I'm not allowed
which makes me want to go there even more,
see those lovely hands oil the lingam
as they ready their lord for bed.

Balancing Act

I just trusted my body,
bent it back like a wave
about to come in, unstressed.
One thing taut, the rope I was learning.
I dusted my feet with turmeric,
wrapped my head in muslin,
practised holding a length of gold bamboo.

The quiet surface of the sole of my foot
met twisted skein stretched out,
destination, lover with blue umbrella.
I just trusted my body
as I felt my way, toes first,
not knowing how far
or how long endurance was.
I feared the rope might snap
like a piece of charcoal –
can rope be over-tensioned?

My tongue was on the roof of my mouth,
I was blindfolded,
palms gripped the smoothness of bamboo –
it can grow over a metre a day,
over-extending itself
the way I thought I was.
I just trusted my body
and it took me straight to you,
your cobalt silk umbrella
matches your eyes, I saw that

as I stripped off my blindfold
threw down the bamboo,
pressed my feet on ricepaper
leaving yellow footprints
as a sign that I tightrope walked
across the temple tank to you.

Girl Almost Writing

I clicked on the menu hoping Mila, Anne,
Pascale might offer up a line or two,
free up my pencil which hovered
like a bee cooling her wings.
They lend me ready-made themes:
my mirror is not mute, blurts out
whatever it thinks,
reflects back freckles where there are none.

Husbands barge into your dreams
in their heavy suits and boots like hooves
kicking the bars of their cage.
Zoos breed neurotic behaviours;
pacing, self-harm,
and sudden eruptions of violence
like the elephant who crushed its
keeper's face with a foot.

In her concrete pit at the zoo, a polar bear
paced back and forth dreaming of fishing holes
in imaginary ice, a husband, a drop in temperature.
It was summer in the house of my past
where I discovered mirrors make fine ponds
for miniature gardens, surrounded them with moss.
Husbands cut lawns as if shaving beards,
they return like the stamping of an elephant's foot
as it baulks at captivity.

Girl Dogging

On my way to the shops I pass two pairs of abandoned shoes,
pink satin little girls' shoes, soft and pliable
with embroidered flowers and buttoned straps,
shoes for a soft instep,
dancer, acrobat, tightrope walker?

Behind the shopfront a man and a woman
move in slow motion –
he presses his chest into her back
brings his hands round to her breast, her throat,
as she tilts her head to receive his kiss
on her neck.

A man and a woman lost
at the footing of a wall in a car park.
He pushes himself into her,
they listen to each others' breath
and also the trickle of water into a stone trough.
She shuts her eyes, is limp and weak
and the buttress screened them
from the comings and goings of the car park,
cascade of empty bottles,
revving of a four by four,
espresso machine in the café.

Girl Reading At Window

I'm sitting in my favourite window-seat
curled up on cushions
with my boots laced up to my knees,
a dress of yellow organdie.
Behind me or in front,
depending on your point of view,
the sea, pale as English seas are,
with churned up sand and limpets
holding fast to rocks.
Reading, reading, causes
wardresses in black taffeta to appear
and *ma poupée* with her beak and talons,
a man in top hat and riding boots
with a nasty looking dog on a chain
whose bark amplifies in the cold chimneys.
It's summer but the rain comes down in sheets
and blurs the pane, makes watermarks
on the silk aprons of the women
growing larger by the second –
they've burst out of their shoes
and let their bulbous toes spread out
on the turkey carpet on which
they plant themselves like trees.
They dress me up in front of the looking glass
but I flounce to the other side of the mirror
where I practise some unusual selves:
painter, pastry-cook, dog-handler,
mountaineer, traveller.

Girl In Sandpit

Sleep is punctured by solar flares,
violent illuminations that hijack you
in your state of least resistance.

Beyond you is the new summerhouse
lit by the kind of light you crave
as you go pale behind windows
whose panes are sealed with lead.

Someone shouts for you as if her life
depends on your intercession,
holds up a glass of liquid sapphire;
essence of bitter orange clarified,
becoming ever more blue.

In the bottom of her glass a small self's voice
cracks like ice. It's your daughter,
marooned on polar ice without proper equipment.
Only ribbons, elastic, raffia….

She wills herself back to the sandpit,
she sieves, scoops, sifts,
makes an imprint of her foot
at seven years old.

One sandpit leads to another:
step into a world of your own making
peopled with holy men, flying trunks,
magic carpets and some pyramids.

You knew the desert would be like this
as you wrap muslin round your face
because sand storms are imminent.

Your drink sits on your father's
copper tray from Persia.
Our father, which art in… exactly.

A whole dinner hour passes
at the oasis nibbling glace dates,
applying henna to your feet.

Home time and when you take off
your bar shoes and socks
out trickles a stream of sand,
insects' wings, hands praying.

Girl Lifting Skirt to Dog
for Paula Rego

Slowly I lift my skirt, my matador's cape,
part of my suit of lights in which I ape
teasing him with what I don't know I have:
an orchid peeping from black foliage,
or ipomoeas on the rampage
when Dog plunges his wet nose in,
relieves his pricked up ears of fleas
crazed by blood, my own grazed knees.

Girl Swimming

Aegean lures, irresistible blues,
palette of silver light waits for a brush
with bodies fresh off the plane
coming out from under their cloud cover
into an insistent sunlight.
I took the girl to water and she swam!
She swims, despite multiple jellyfish stings,
she's snorkelling, truffling down through bubbles
to find her crimson starfish.

Our strokes evenly matched
we plough on right to the harbour's mouth
is it safe out there?
All wet lip, pearls for teeth,
we run our tongues over their rippled surface,
smooth but not symmetrical
like her foot, the one with the twist
that makes her even more your own.

You can barely hear spoons rattle
you're out so far. Only the music
of swallows' wings zigzagging across the bay
in a dazzle of metallic blue reaches your ears.
The slow swim back towards land
calls us back into voice and air.
We're losing our winter pallor,
cherries are in season.

Finding Your Place

Happens, now you can jettison
search engine, restlessness,
settle in to your place like an old shoe,
follow the island's every inlet,
map its entirety in your head.
Your place's lexicon
is much reduced
as if you were boiling sauce on a high heat
left with concentrate,
blend of essential flavours
strong on your tongue.
Mountain (you have to have at least one)
Monastery (peak sanctuary if you're Minoan)
Caique (public transport from one inlet to another)
Coffee (Greek of course, and medium sweet)
Omelette (a special one with feta cheese)
Olive (pre-eminent tree, liquid light)
Maquis (infusion of herb).
You tumble the words around
like gemstones being polished up.
Stripped down, pared away,
a few cotton shirts, a pencil and notebook,
swimming things and mobile phone.
You could lose your place
but it will always find you:
it's bookmarked,
one click and you're there.

A Passing Phase

Slick as moonlight on water
she shoots out of me like a star
in the moon-sterile room
where newborns introduce themselves
to mothers whose craters gape
before they're sewn up tight
for their husbands.
Her foot's a crescent,
mirrors my own moon
hung in the hospital window
making instruments gleam.

Full moon, python of the threshold,
dead birds in the chimney.
I throw his cigarettes away
under a smoker's moon, nicotine yellow,
probing the body for bronchioles.
Must give up, it's an issue,
rotten tissue, scarred and tarred.
Would you like one? Can I cadge one?
Every quarter I've predicted
we'll fall out over this.

The moon was either new or dark
on our second meeting by water
where we craned our necks
to watch meteors sear
through Perseus. Gone in a blink.
Ingested light. Plasma music.

We shift our gaze from long shot
to close-up; fall into each other's orbit,
drown in one of those gravid seas:
Maria, dark area,
side of ourselves we've yet to discover.

Farouche

I introduce myself to you,
we converse in Portuguese.
I copy Celestina in her black dress
and pointy dancing shoes:
hair drawn back in a bun
tightens skin on cheekbones.

Displayed on a platform
we become public property,
our every attempt
to negotiate a cramped geometry
is noted, catalogued.

You tell me, in broken English,
that we are in rotation.
So, a physicist lover!
But I have a blind spot for science,
prefer stories, lies,
ideal forms and structures
with pleats and darts,
invisible hems like skirts.

We assume we are farouche,
at least ambivalence
performs its subtle dialogue.
Incarceration makes us ponder
how we have become
each other's analgesic,
a nuance of pain deadened

right in front of the audience
who take us for ornaments,
life-sized but evidently breakable.

Eight hours of close proximity
tests our tolerance.
If only I had a paper fan
with which to feign privacy.

We have to re-compose ourselves,
rewrite, revise our adherence
to either / or, relinquish roles
we took to be irreversible.

Bushcraft

When we came back from the bush
with our tinderboxes in leather pouches
I was able to answer the question
posed many months before –
How is it that your love
burns just as bright
as the day you kindled it?
So many people's fires are out.

Proximity, the familiar scent of your skin
is enough to startle fire from its embers
which glow, imperceptibly
at subcutaneous level, sending smoke signals
that get us rummaging
in the paraphernalia of fire building,
our treasured tinderbox,
hazina. You are my hazina, treasure,
that African word the guide taught us
which has doubled, trebled, multiplied,
each time our bodies meet,
and each time anticipate another,
and another…..

We're oblivious to the possibility
of flame retardant or total quenching.
Friction is our language,
friction that elicits smoke,
then magics up a tiny flame,

telling us we've become practised
pyromaniacs.

We couldn't get used to our house,
dragged a mattress onto the lawn
to lie on our backs and gaze at stars
the way we had in the wilderness
a campfire at our feet,
the crackle and glow of fire
never more sweet.

Sweet Doing Nothing

We place a mirror
which lets the ocean in

to scatter salt on our bedcover,
watch crystals deliquesce
let's bake a dover

sole! I dab saffron on your lip,
you can taste paella
bubbling in its cartwheel pan,

we put pepper in our shoes
tickle our insteps.
Stand on tiptoe, refuse

to forget our friend
who calls the horizon
virgin of wounded handkerchiefs

his special talent
for dolour, we forever
try to lift

with our swimming expeditions
and simple tasks –
we set him to caulk the boat with tar

which made him dream up soil
and black ponies,
their hooves dipped in crude oil

letting a slick of it careen,
seep from holding tanks
to subdue the colour aquamarine.

Pollution is ever in his mind's eye,
come, let's light a small fire
for cooking langoustines

allow salt and lemon juice
to bathe your fingers
before you let your pen loose

to celebrate retreat of ponies,
erasure of future time
with some *dolce far niente*

or sweet doing nothing
that spells darkness,
sun inexorably slipping.

Scalded

My search for some leitmotif
ends with the idea of quarantine,
it synchronises with a depth-charge
detonated by an awful thump
deep inside my body. Its message
of *too much, or, not enough*
makes me steady myself on my spade
whose blade's firmly entrenched
in newly turned soil.

Alert as a bird in danger
I listen, watch myself fly back
from Port Lligat near Cadaques,
with its pine tree grown in an old boat –
pinioned, earthed.

The Tramontana got hysterical
as we walked over the hill
past giant egg and crude pitchfork
tuning in to dangerous weather.
No-one can eat outside,
the wind tears food from your plate,
snatches our voices away from us,
fills the space between your mouth and mine
with smoke and seaspray.

Fuente

The lemon tree is a pip spit away in the walled garden
and always a woman in black sweeps the street clean
after a hundred goats pass by on their way to be milked –
six o'clock by goat bell music
which prompts Rosaria to remind her husband to wash.

My rug is a Marsh Arab ceremonial blanket
of embroidered wool whose colours stay bright:
orange, purple, red, pink.

Rosaria's out in the street now
talking to herself below my balcony,
warning us, points up with her finger – *el sol, el sol, el sol*....
and she walks on the shadowed side of the street
past the village laundry sinks
where water comes straight from the mountains,
snow-melt, *agua sana, buena, buena.*

I fill my bottle from the spout,
carry it back to our house, a gift.

Gacela For The Life Of Julia

Eviction. Shut out of her own house
with only a *Life of Lorca*
for company.

Her scribbled margin note,
beside *given lots of coffee,*
explains the code they used
for disappearing all the ones

who troubled them, refused
to toe the line, like Julia,
fearless in the face of swift decline.

What we learn in the dark
flattens, lightens
to the weight of a feather
from one of her beloved doves.

My mentor found and lost,
lost then found again
in all the colours she wore, wrote,
corresponded with.

How much, without light,
she resembles a white
camellia bud,
               frosted.

Silk Purse

I had to take the knife and slit her throat
watch as all her body's blood drained slowly
out into the bowl. The very bowl I found

in pieces on the floor, a broken boat,
not watertight but leaky.
I had to take the knife and slit her throat,

my own heart beating in my stapled throat
for all the slaughtered beasts drained carefully
out into the bowl. The very bowl found

in amongst some rusty pans and old coats,
their owners disappeared – occluded sky.
I had to take the knife and slit her throat,

mix in cinnamon, pimiento, oat,
become a morcillera with my spici-
ness into the bowl. The very bowl found

in two, cracked glaze, split pomegranate;
fruit that lent its name to hand weaponry.
I had to take the knife and slit her throat,
out into the bowl. That bright bowl I found.

Allotment

In one leaf of cavolo nero
there's a landscape (Tuscan), a relief
map giving me the what's beneath
and least thought of, the skeletal,
right down to what they call the sacred bone.

We meet at a restaurant – Carluccio's –
she's wearing dark red trousers,
my hands rest on her shoulder blades,
her scapulae, which makes her shed a few tears
but I never found out what for
as we're moments away from a bottle of wine,
a shift of mood, sadness fades.

I show her my painting,
out of darkness into light,
an emblem for us both
as the old door swings open,
lets us into sunlight, drives away
a chill that's been too long in our bones.

We come across some baby cavolo nero,
tiny plumes on a strong stem,
praise green, attend the season's necessity,
make soup, thick, filling soup
with freshly grated parmesan
long matured in its ageing room
like a holy relic, saint's bone.

Aperture
after James Turrell

He parcels up the sky
with one simple device,
an open skylight that tunnels,
funnels our vision upwards
to a square in which swallows fly
and cloud parades across blue.
He talks of harvesting galactic light,
old light and its chronology.

His ambition is to mesmerise.
You sit. I sit. We crane our necks,
occupy unforgiving seats,
a ceremonial, devotional furniture
that helps us apprehend unfurnished sky.
Dusk. I count seven stars.
They appear one by one,
sudden apparitions.

You're restless, go back outside
the deer shelter, stamp your hooves,
rub your antlers on a lintel.

Attention-seeking

Effortlessly, instinctively, my hibiscus
unfurls her new petals
wet as wings
which shiver; the sun
is not out. She shakes a crimson
ribbon out of the heart of her, vital
and loud it sings,
calls to me as I'm down on my knees,
makes me turn, respond to a ruse
I did not believe I'd fall
for. Uncanny thing
this flower, powerful as discus
hurled, landing, purring
sound of hibiscus flexing her mettle.

High Tea

Each influx huddles in the valley,
it bulges, distends, a seedpod
ripe for dispersal
followed by heavy precipitation
and the reflex action of gutter and drain.

Grit silts up spout,
      clear your throat, spit.
Drizzle on sheep's wool,
windscreen wipers full on. Lit
up trig point accessible only on foot
earns you the right to sit
among bushes yielding indigo
smears for your lip
      coming across tiny storms
in teacups. Spoonful of upland pollen.

Each influx disbelieves
its loss of light,
must be someone else's weather
coming in like an uninvited guest.
Cloud thickens, drops,
introduces flood to the town's vocabulary
together with drown, and rat.

You have to equip yourself
with waterproof everything,
haul yourself up beyond any boundary,
experience what unfenced feels like

and later, as the boiler fires up
your central heating, think about
the word indigenous,
and what you're not – your vowels
not flat enough,
your felt skirt only an affectation.

Sharon Olds Reads To The Animals

Over skeletons, over blind animals
with their smell of taxidermy,
hangs a glass box, a vivarium,
whose curator is expert in heat and light,
especially light. Her voice rises,
illumines every situation, commands attention
the way only someone from the ministry of bone can.

She quickens your senses till your body's steam-cleaned
like a cared-for house where
a polished rustle of python skin
is shiny with introduced light,
and splayed leaves press against their panes,
jealous of you, left to your own devices
in that hall of bone where a human skeleton
all wired-up, swims, swims,
but never reaches the bank of any river
or the shore of any ocean.

Bone, skin, pelt, hoof,
among an audience to which I belong,
listening to the woman read from her book
whose moleskin cover's soft in her hand;
it tells me how to live, how she lives,
how I could live, fully alert to blood and flesh:
she's a struck match, kindling.

Picking Glasswort

> "half way down
>   hangs one that gathers samphire;
>   dreadful trade"
>   *King Lear*

Half way down my road to recovery
I pick samphire, glasswort,
you can recover its sodium if you burn it;
it's therapeutic, tonic, excellent with fish.

Half way to a half- life of decay
I contemplate what tides can do
to blood and brain, incidental,
say the word cerebellum out loud.

Half way to the horizon
I catch sight of St Elmo's Fire,
blue plasma, night's phosphorescence,
storm barometer that rescues me.

Half way through my story,
its pull and push,
its impulse linear towards an end
is a tug of war between water and sand dune

which I'm half way down,
my bare feet half buried
in whispering sands, silica,
the kind that brush particles together.

It's half-light, neither day nor night,
a cormorant takes its first fish,
my fire on the beach smoulders,
lends me a little warmth before the sun rises.

Postcard From The Zone

Intellectually I enter it
but in practice, hardly ever do,
stuck on the threshold,
tentative opening of window –
French, with its long pane
of famously unstable
supercooled liquidity

which masquerades as solid
as the stone steps
where yesterday I found
scraps of broken mirror
and *needle to sea bottom*
approximates the feeling
a sliver of sky has
when pinned like a moth
inside its collector's cabinet.

Stork Cools Wings

The crimson legs of storks stream out
as they fly in
from Sinai to Gabel El Zeit.
Imperial red wanes,

occupation just a cheap trick.
Guano. The stork does not like her nest
colonised, her feet thrash and kick,
demand some self-determination.

Regime change, history's tendency
prevails again,
in our own time fifty years hence.
The valve house remains,

its Egyptian style of dressed stone
leans towards a non-
existent stand of acacia;
the stork's favourite nesting site.

Here, beside six
hundred and thirty three
million gallons of drinking water
the Scots Pine falters,

bent by wind that brings geese
home from their long flight south.
They celebrate
by much grooming of feathers.

Each time I practise *stork cools wings*
I'm fanned by thermals from the Red Sea,
drop beak: *needle to sea bottom.*

Paper Wings
after Bill Viola 'The Passions' – *Catherine's Room* (2001)

As happens in libraries, circus rings,
you get over-exposed to light,
accessing unspoken, unbroken timelines.
Away in a room on a mountain
time is measured by sunlight
feeling its way along a branch of almond blossom
like an arm leaning across the window frame
trying to get inside.

Writing takes up two whole hours;
mechanical, precise as clockwork
or ragged as an unravelling skein.
When light eventually dwindles
I light all the candles with a beeswax taper,
flood myself with candlelight,
soft, like wings or quilts.
The flowering branch becomes a silhouette,
a negative space by which I define its shape
(and my own). Replete with solitude
I climb into bed where my sense of self
is either magnified or reduced.

Tomorrow will be much the same
petals a little more open
page with its extended lines
leads to the high waterfall known as Angel,

whose waters I collect in a glass vial
to sip in the small hours when sleep eludes me
and sun is yet to rise on its paper wings
to remake mountain, woman, almond branch.

In flight from an excess of news
your wings develop complicated markings
like those animals in zoos
divorced from mate, habitat, clues
to what and who they are.

A Barefoot Doctor Asks Me To Undress

"shed your clothes like pointless wings.
Now it's just the weight of you."
　　　　　　　Michael Symmons Roberts

Of course you have to have the word *sublime*,
transcendent too, contingent on a mountain
with a waterfall in some exotic clime.

No interface to block the light that shines
on every pore – you've shed scraps of lycra,
let sunlight saunter up your spine,

shifting like a desert dune
blown into new topographies,
worn smooth, polished as a spoon.

Huerta de San Vicente

How the kitchen sings
its hollow, polished, beaten melody.

As I peel oranges, a burst of oil
sprays my skin, uncontrollable as dreams.

Jasmine contorts itself into a question –
how is it that unravelling is so irresistible?

Newly spun cotton woven into a bedspread
embroidered with two-headed birds;
flights of turquoise, scarlet, emerald.

Pith on the table is an avalanche;
white as medulla, essential
like blood or lymph.

A Single Orange Was The Only Light

Time change, its arbitrary gain
fastens shutters tight,
keeps out a curl of rind that is the moon:
clotted cream on sugar cane.

Me, you, our iron bed. You say my name,
we've a single orange for galvanisation.
Suspiro! The night air a warm lagoon,
smell of orange blossom like a tisane.

Suddenly we're in a hurry,
water in its channel released
after being held behind a gate,
eager to rush and tumble.

It's late. We are two halves cleaving,
sticky, squeezed out,
we stay in bed till noon
in our casita under a mountain.

We make an orange and almond tart, spoon,
beat, fold, bake, till it's burnished frangipane,
sun rising.

Notes

p. 37 'Cuckoo': 'Some Questions You Might Ask' from *House of Light*, 1990, by Mary Oliver.

p. 42 'Rosita Rules The Roost': *give me an orange or a good quince any day, / and you can keep all the roses in the world* from 'Dona Rosita' by Federico Garcia Lorca.

p. 46 'Bitter Water': *lungi* – loincloth worn by Indian men.

p. 73 'Gacela For The Life Of Julia': *given lots of coffee (dale café, mucho café)* was the code used by the military who assassinated Lorca.

p. 84 'Stork Cools Wings': *stork cools wings* and *needle to sea bottom* are tai chi positions.

Biographical Note

LIZ ALMOND was born in Newcastle-upon-Tyne, grew up in South London, and has lived for many years in Hebden Bridge. She has taught Creative Writing at Manchester Metropolitan University's Alsager Faculty and at the University of Huddersfield.

Yelp! is her second collection of poems to be published, her first collection, *The Shut Drawer*, appearing in 2002 from Arc.

Recent titles in Arc Publications'
POETRY FROM THE UK / IRELAND,
include:

LIZ ALMOND
The Shut Drawer

JONATHAN ASSER
Outside The All Stars

DONALD ATKINSON
*In Waterlight: Poems New,
Selected & Revised*

JOANNA BOULTER
*Twenty Four Preludes & Fugues
on Dmitri Shostakovich*

THOMAS A CLARK
The Path to the Sea

TONY CURTIS
*What Darkness Covers
The Well in the Rain*

JULIA DARLING
*Sudden Collapses in Public Places
Apology for Absence*

CHRIS EMERY
*Dr. Mephisto
Radio Nostalgia*

KATHERINE GALLAGHER
Circus-Apprentice

CHRISSIE GITTINS
Armature

MICHAEL HASLAM
*The Music Laid Her Songs in
Language
A Sinner Saved by Grace*

BRIAN JOHNSTONE
The Book of Belongings

JOEL LANE
Trouble in the Heartland

HERBERT LOMAS
The Vale of Todmorden

PETE MORGAN
August Light

MICHAEL O'NEILL
Wheel

IAN POPLE
An Occasional Lean-to

PAUL STUBBS
The Icon Maker

SUBHADASSI
peeled

LORNA THORPE
A Ghost in My House

MICHELENE WANDOR
*Musica Transalpina
Music of the Prophets*

JACKIE WILLS
*Fever Tree
Commandments*